Haiku From the Heart

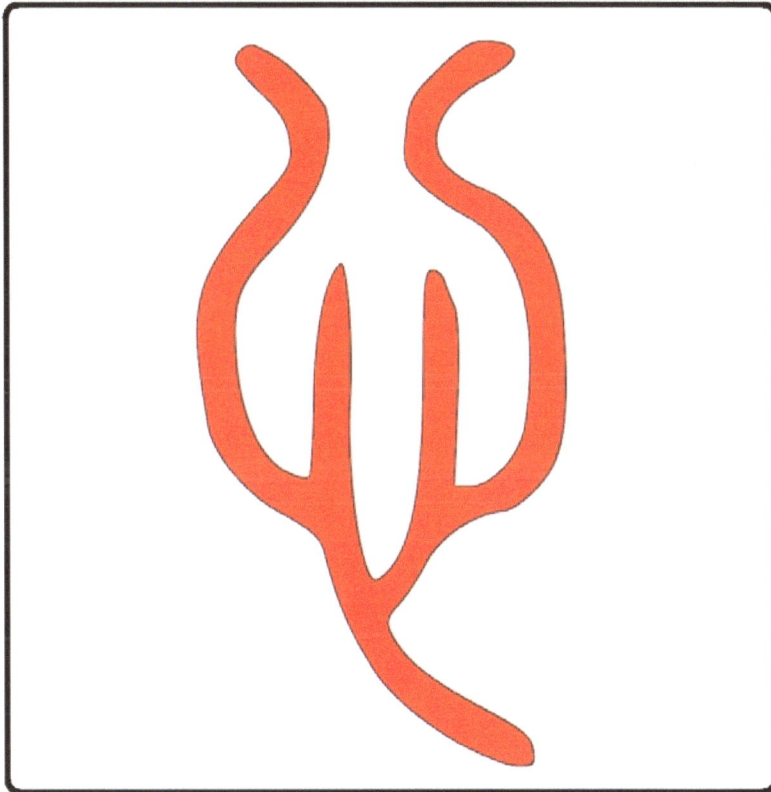

J G Lynn

Nian Media

Nian Brands Corporation

Wilmington, Delaware

ISBN 978-0692596548

First Edition

To Karen

who inspires my heart

Contents

Preface

This book is about connections. It's about the connections we make with places, it's about the connections we make with people; it's about the connections we make with events in our life.

Traditional Japanese *haiku* is a short form of poetry which consists of seventeen syllables in three phrases which consist of five, seven, and five syllables, for a total of seventeen syllables. The three phrases are traditionally written on three lines. The rhythm falls accordingly into the three phrases as in:

One two three four five

One two three four, five six sev

One two three four five

A haiku typically has the characteristic known as *kiru*, or cutting. The haiku will start by reflecting one thought and then "cut" to another, often pivoting on a single word or syllable.

In modern times, especially in America, haiku is defined more loosely. It may have less than seventeen syllables and is often written on one line, three, or even in a circle. I have settled on my own understanding of haiku as a form of poetry which is terse and concise, attempting to catch the essence of a feeling, mood, or situation while working within certain rules, sometimes bending them but not breaking them. The evolution of how haiku in modern times seems similar to the changes in the musical world during the Baroque period and the Viennese period (sometimes referred to as the Classical period. During the Baroque period composers followed a rather strict set of rules for their compositions, both in the overall format and in the harmonic structure. Certain things were not allowed, a composer could not move from one note to another if it broke certain rules of harmony. As new composers came along, they didn't throw all of these rules out the window, but they questioned them, made exceptions, and stretched the boundaries of what was considered good harmonic practice. All you have to do is listen to a piece by Bach and a piece by Mozart to hear how different they are. While Bach is incredibly good and progresses with mathematical precision, Mozart eschewed the rigidity in favour of an almost experimental approach to melodic and harmonic progression. For this reason, I feel justified in not holding on too closely to the traditional rules of composing Haiku and instead have chosen to focus on expressing poignant and meaningful thoughts.

When I started writing haiku I only intended to write a few haiku which were meaningful to me. Soon after I began, I had the idea to include pictures which I thought reflected the spirit of each haiku. Later on, I would see something and think to myself, "I should write a haiku about this." I didn't set out to write a book of haiku, but after a while I felt that I should share them in the hopes that some of the thoughts, feelings, and moods might resonate with others. So what I ended up with is a book which is a collection of twenty-two haiku composed during one year, 2015. In hindsight, I wish I had written more during the year. Someday I might try to commit myself to writing one haiku per week. At least then I would know I would have 52 haiku for the year. Remember, this isn't a novel. It isn't a story. There's no rush to get to the end. Although some of the haiku are related, each is meant to stand on its own. If you take the time to read them and ponder them one at a time, you may find that you make connections of your own. I hope you find at least one here that speaks to you.

– J G Lynn

The Sun and Sky

In the morning sun

I see myself;

from within

I can see

the truth.

In the evening sun

    I see the world;

from down here

    I see all

        heaven.

Standing in the rain

I feel renewed;

the water

helps
me
cleanse

my faults.

Watching the snow fall

through the window,

with the wind

blowing through

the trees.

Life in General

Driving through the night

        the day recedes;

up ahead

    she lies in

      my heart.

Tunnel lights are bright,

they wake me up,

for a while —

before I ...

drift off.

Drinking through the night

       my problems fade;

My focus

      ...and balance

         follow.

Singapore Botanic Gardens

Walking to the park

                     to do tai chi;

all of my

          friends will be

                    with me.

Thinking of the past

the years flew by;

I think of

the future

. . . and Cry.

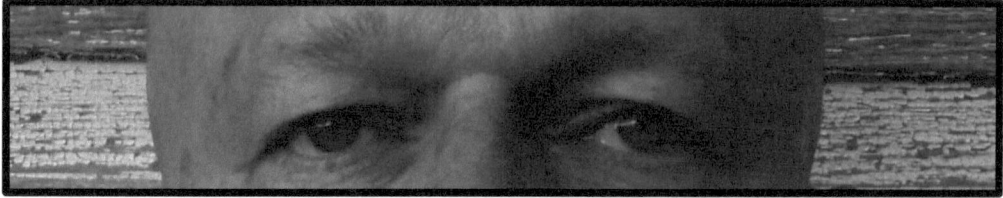

Those last few seconds,

when everyone

has passed on,

while waiting

your turn.

Sunday morning . . . tired . . .

the sun attacks.

My legs and

my shoulders

repose.

The Rest of the World

Downtown Buenos Aires, Argentina

Living on the streets...

Presidenta!

Evita

looks down from

above.

Avenida Atlantica , Rio de Janeiro

Walking down the street

next to the beach;

the natives

ignore my

survey.

Ipanema Beach, Rio de Janeiro

Ipanema beach,

        cloudy today;

keeps away

      all of the

          women.

Sugarloaf Mountain, Rio de Janeiro

Sugarloaf mountain

rises upward;

leaving me

below and

at peace

Sitting on a plane –

flight to japan.

My eyelids

beginning

to shut.

Tokyo Bay

Tokyo at night,

stillness descends;

Excitement

lies dormant

in wait.

Hong Kong

Just imagine that

       all of New York,

has become Chinatown –

          Hong Kong.

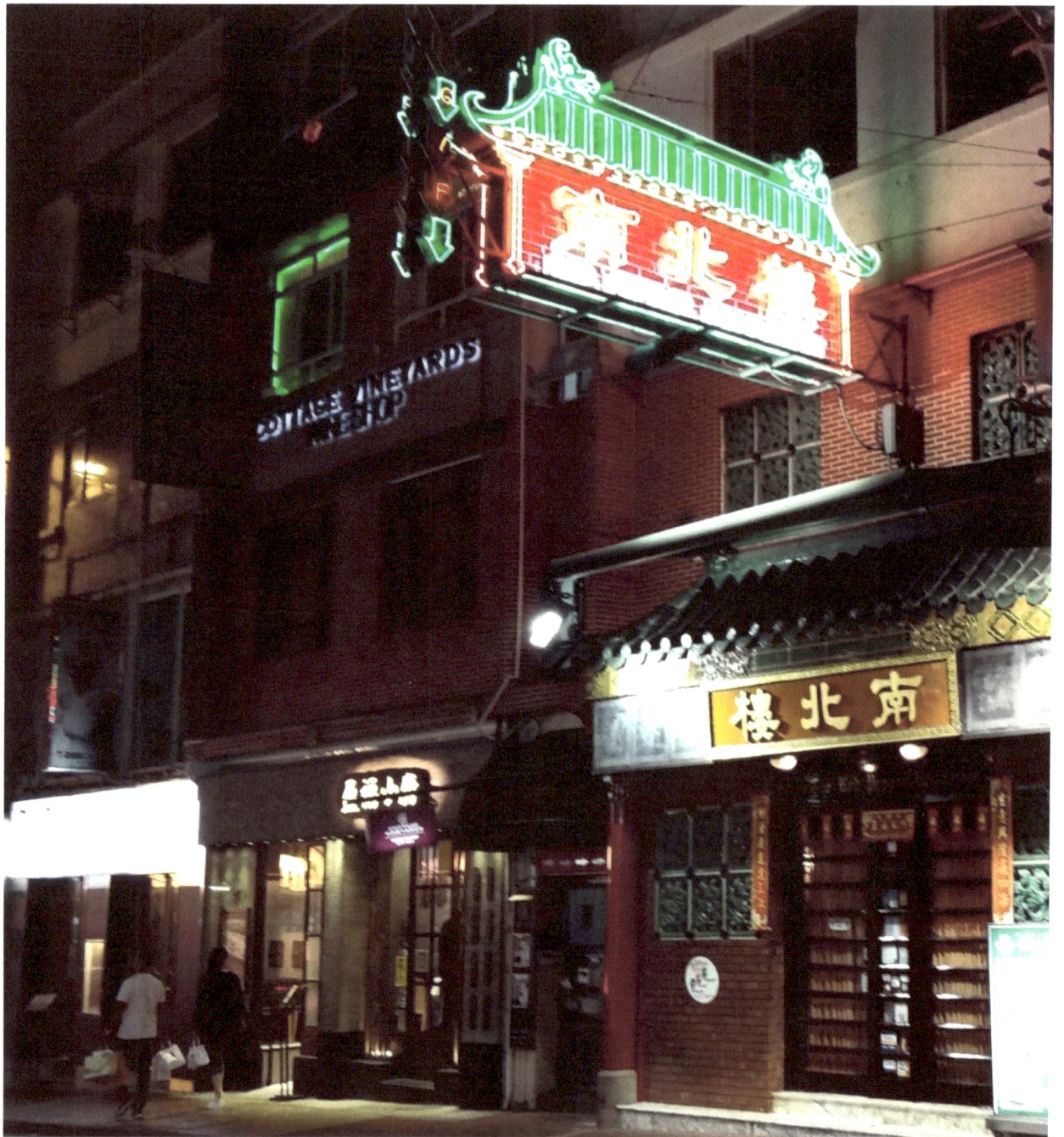

Red Pepper Restaurant, Hong Kong

Hong Kong after dark

the streets come alive;

some of us

will party

'til dawn.

The End of the Year

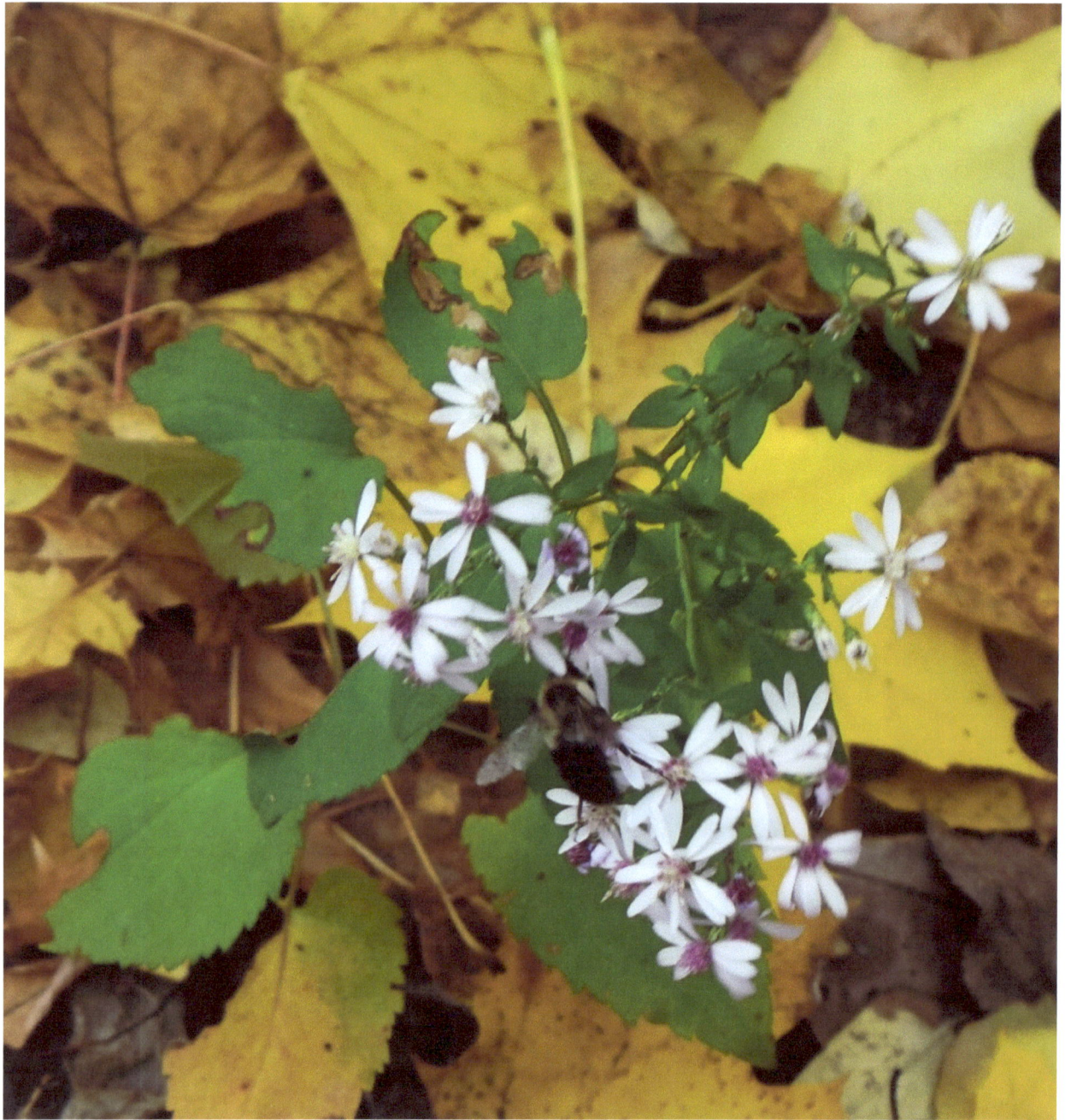

Bumblebees in fall,

            gathering still;

     where do they

           go for the

                 winter?

Day after Christmas,

no snow in sight;

loneliness

creeps into

my heart.

New Year's Day at last,

and last year fades

relaxing,

while planning

the next.

New Year's Day
2009

www.ingramcontent.com/pod-product-compliance
Lightning Source LLC
Chambersburg PA
CBHW041426090426

42741CB00002B/46

* 9 7 8 0 6 9 2 5 9 6 5 4 8 *